Elektra's Mouth

Suzi Kaplan Olmsted

Virgogray Press

VG-38

Cover Images: Suzi Kaplan Olmsted
Illustrations: Marc Olmsted
Cover and Book Design: Michael Aaron Casares

ISBN: 978-1-105-49927-2
Printed at www.lulu.com
Published by Virgogray Press
Austin, TX, United States of America
http://www.virgograypress.com/

Elektra's Mouth

Suzi Kaplan Olmsted

Touchdown Jesus is Gone

It used to be visible for miles,
arms raised toward the heavens,
announcing victory.

Around the Ohio church,
this statue was a landmark.
Area residents enjoyed seeing it
day after day.

"Touchdown" Jesus, they called it.
Highway 75 had little else of note and
 it was always good to be reminded of one's faith.

Lightening struck Jesus' right hand, and he caught fire.

Area resident Cassie Browning tried to reassure,
"The statue of Jesus can be destroyed, but Jesus can't,"
though another resident
who used to stop at the statue
at least once a week
told onlookers,
"I just don't understand what God is up to.
It just doesn't make
any sense."

June 28, 2010

Ash and Bone

Ashlyn laughs
at our desiccated corpses -
Beautiful, juicy, full
of nothing so much as
tomorrow's tomorrows -
Even if we know the secrets of history
right now history only runs forward,
made by luscious 17-year-olds
who know more than
we have ever asked -
& leaving farewell kisses on her
we who love her,
who made her,
offer our bones for her to eat.

6.2.2010

I am a Child of Pyschotherapists

Trained and educated as a therapist, myself
Really, really trained and educated,when I decided to set it aside
It required explanation when I didn't want
To be a participant in therapy myself
On either side
I gave a lot of explanations
but none of them were true
not because I was lying,
but because I was unable to say what was true at the time
I had a whole series of therapists, one after another
some of them proclaimed otherwise
but none of them believed in things that go bump in the night
In evil, and horrible, unexpected, undeserved tragedy, without reason
or a lesson, or animals with souls, or plain old bad guys
I had a male therapist that thought I was just being guarded and anxious
Men were no cause for concern
A statement which isn't even true for men
Who seem to constantly bonk each other on the head for money, land, religion
or just because they want to,
let alone for the want of women
That very handsome male therapist
didn't think women should worry,
life wasn't a cautionary tale
We got on well otherwise,
but he determined my evaluation of the danger in the world,
rather than an accurate evaluation of the nature of things,
a reason to recommend more therapy,
for me,I stead of the world
In the way joints squeak without oil,

and landlords demand rent and extra (wink, wink - all pretty girls understand),
the rich get all kinds of things for free
while the poor pay double and more
no one likes an empty pocket,
and no one should go hungry to the store
hard work can pull one up with one's bootstraps
if one has money from someone's dad as well
but just working hard because you're trapped,
well, then you'll have to work more
The bumps in the night are the stomachs of girls with no choice
and call them what you want,
unwilling's unwilling, and a child is doubly poor.
My friends speak often to cats and dogs,
Know that things go bump in the night
& fight demons*every single day

Oakland Dentist

Gold teeth in front
Bullet hole in the window
The receptionist wore slippers

Pink Tutu, Green Sweatpants

Perfect San Francisco Sunday morning
park shining January cold
little Albert toddles away
from his mother
with pink tutu over green sweatpants
Mom gently calls
no Albert no
we're not doing that now
come back here
pink tutu over green sweatpants
still flying away
on tiny legs
sweet, sweet, mommy no

1/5/03

Homeless Sacrament

Reading Harpers
lovely sad piece
about a guy with a parking lot
who doesn’t drive -
homeless people
camp there
the police come up with
reasons
excuses
possible ordinances
so they can kick the
people off

The Love Bug

In Memory Buddy Hackett 1924-2003

I was six years old. It was our first Halloween in Beverly Hills. My father owned a local toy store and I was dressed in the clothes off my life-sized Raggedy Anne doll. My mother had made me a wig and done the make-up. My parents were going out with new Beverly Hills friends and so was I.

I was dropped off with some strange parents and a large group of kids to patrol the foreign neighborhood for treats. I was lost almost at once.

I found myself in front of a large corner house all alone, no kids, no parents in sight. An enormous stone elephant greeted all visitors to the house. So I went to the door.

It was there that Buddy Hackett found me. Not Herbie the Love Bug man as I knew him even though the fog of my lost six-year-old fear and remaining lust for candy. No, this was slick, Dean Martinesque Buddy Hackett, wearing a groovy 1968 suit and hip shoes and tinted glasses at night and a highball in his hand, after an unsuccessful call to my parents.

Buddy Hackett sat down and watched the Disney movie on TV with me, gracefully acting like his only plan for the evening was to drink highballs with Raggedy Anne and watch TV while elegantly dressed, though he was still the funny guy from *The Love Bug* to my thrilled six-year-old brain.

The Milk of Human Kindness

I'm walking in the rain on the way to work
Exhausted, with a terrible cough
Thinking about how hard it is
Carrying all these dark stories
Accumulated in my head
Building up a mountain of pain
This morning on the news they announced
A new game show
Whoever can spend a million dollars
In less than half an hour
With no notice
Just getting a call from Donald Trump
Spending every penny completely before another half hour has passed
Gets to keep it
I walk all the way to work
Thinking I know exactly how to win this game
Give all the money away
Every penny
Thinking about the people who
Like me
Carry around years and years of horror stories in their heads
And don't get paid enough to live in the city where they work
I wonder how much you actually have to get paid to keep
Feeling okay about this
To not want to cry when they talk about their parents raping them
To still have more than a glimmer of hope when you see their kids in tow
Learning the same things, the same way, or even harder
I figure out a scheme so I can give the money away and still get the taxes paid
And not have the money pissed away by the stupidity of
The helper's money people
But I'm thinking about just how stupid I know they can be
And a man in very elegant rags swoops up on me in the rain
We are alone on the sidewalk in the light rain
He has made a sign on a square of used cardboard

But he says the same thing verbally
“I’m looking for the milk of human kindness.”
“I’m running a little short on human kindness today.”
He says he really just needs a cup of coffee
I don’t get him that either

There is a Place I can Stand

Where I am beautiful and every pair of pants fits me
Where my airplane is parked next to me
And there are no soldiers because as president
I'd make war illegal
And as a doctor I'd cure cancer
And as a scientist I'd feed the world
In between all the movies in which I starred
And the records with my singing
There is a place to stand
Where I am seven years old
And the piano is easy
And so is walking on my hands
We'll all spend part of every day
Upside down
Walking on our hands
Then doing somersaults
Cartwheels and flips
There is a place
Where I have never cried
Over anything worse
Than losing my friend Renna's
Rabbit fur glove
And the worst thing I've ever done
Is hiding peas in my napkin
At Heidi Slate's house
And where I am sure
That I'm safe
From a vampire attack
As long as the blanket
Is pulled up
To my chin

The Russian

She is the only Jewish child in the South Milwaukee neighborhood. By 1945 her brother, born of the same parents in Wisconsin, has convinced everyone outside the family that he is not Jewish, he is Russian, so only she is chased home, ducking the projectiles of whatever the neighborhood children can find, bottles, rocks, vegetables, calling her a dirty Jew.

Not too dirty to touch. Even at nine years old, she is beautiful. She has blond hair and almond shaped eyes that seem knowing, though what they might know can be left up to some debate. She has the slashing high cheekbones of a Tartar ancestor who passed through on one Pogrom or many, and the long delicate neck that would plague her with pain her whole life, too graceful for the heft of her head, full of other places and a life where your best friend's family doesn't kill the pet rabbit for dinner.

Her brother, the Russian, sees her beauty, sees his friends see her beauty, sees her glow against a backdrop of chicken shit, tin sheds, and milking cows. Gets told how brilliant he is, how he will flower, is the hope of the family. She is not useful. Forced to sit on her left hand so she will not shame them by using it instead of the proper right. The Russian thinks of great things. Those great things include the prepubescent curve of her flank, the promise of her already tiny waist and slightly flared hips. Long legs and graceful ankles. They share a room. She gets up before everyone else so she can be alone in the bathroom for hours, but he sees.

He imagines moving from his bed into hers. He has a great imagination. He is a god, willing things from his imagination to manifest before him. He has made himself Russian. He will lie beside her. He will bring his hands along her smooth, cool skin, slightly damp but still soothing, nectarine kept out of the summer sun in this Midwestern town. He brings his hand to the lop-eared bunny fold of the unformed meeting between her legs, he forces himself in. He is big, hulking, she is young, small. It is the beginning of many such displays of his godly power.

He is a man of ideas. A precursor of the Russian mob. He begins to charge his friends, and older boys, to caress her, to poke at her, to ignore her pleas. She is chattel to the mob, their parents just dirty jews, his friends giant vicious Poles built for meat-packing or steelyards, though they were also just young boys. A world away it was 1945 and her Uncle Moshe was just back, a young soldier and liberator of Dachau. An integral part of Eastern European loathing of Jews, Dachau, part of the apogee of centuries of attempts to tear Poland's Jews limb from limb. A Jew-hating Pole, however young, was no simple thing.

She is strong. She is brave. She will not be chattel. She will not turn to the Jews. She will not fight the Poles. She will go to her teacher, a kind woman, who lets her finish a sentence and gives her books to read. All kinds of books. After hearing the story of the Russian and the Poles, the teacher walks the long-necked girl home, solemnly, in silence, holding her hand all the way, though nine is far too old to require a hand, however long or perilous the walk.

Not a Ballerina

My soft ass presses against red velvet seat
Floppy thighs spread trying not to touch the stranger at my side
Dancers float without effort
Legs lifted defying physics in their own zero gravity
Nutcracker fairies float, and I sink deeper into my own lost plans
Once held before ballet class as an exemplar of perfect ballet feet
I groan quietly as I can as I get up for intermission

Funeral

Driving through the hot December San Fernando Valley
I pass several car carriers full of newly minted baby Mercedes
Shiny and fresh, perfect
Then I get stuck for miles behind
another carrier
a jaguar convertible,
with a giant bucket holding disconnected parts on its back seat
old Volkswagen engine cover lodged firmly into its own bumper, Datsuns,
Hondas, and other cars that would never be whole again
a dull sheen in the southern California sun
headed for the crusher
the driver in no hurry to get them anywhere
I choose not to pass, turning on my headlights, joining the procession

Bu-Ba Image
& Beauty
Super Center
LAW&ORDER:LA
Bu-Ba Image
& Beauty
Super Center
A & W BBQ
& Seafood
Reseda Blvd
Chevron

On the Missing Law & Order: LA Episode

"Osama & Obama
stole 'Reseda' but
we got it back."

Vagina Tears

pussy power
vagina tears
Sister Spit won't call
I am spewing vomit
No snatch-smack for me.*

*oxytocin

Jenette Bras

Bras are not just places we put our boobs
so many names for them
tits melons tatas
I woke up one morning to the news
that a bra would be accompanying me on the rest of my journey
day bras, convertible bras, sexy bras, utilitarian bras, sport bras,
comfy bras, bras for sleep and for sex and bras that hurt my neck,
and bras that leave red angry marks where they used to be
or they would, if I ever took them off
I went topless once at a sunny Southern California party
when I was 19
everyone else was running around freed from the confines of clothes
I thought I'd give it a shot
I sunburned my nipples
I never sun anything
I hate the sun
Now I'll get skin cancer on my jugs hooters boobies
cause everyone was doing it
Jenette is a success, if you want to be a working actor
She works and works –
from my bed I can see her face on my husband's vampire movie poster
not her only significant role
she was a senior when I was a freshman, and I don't feel like we're old
but Hollywood, demon town, East, West or Other
treats her like an old lady now
I gasped the last time I saw her in a movie
Since then I saw her in her eponymous Hollywood lingerie store
fitting a reality show actress with her first bra
she probably doesn't look much older than I do
but I like to think she does

and now, she could fit a bra for me
tell me how it looks
(but I would never ask her)

**Jenette Goldstein of "Near Dark" -*
Jenette Bras is actually the name of her store.

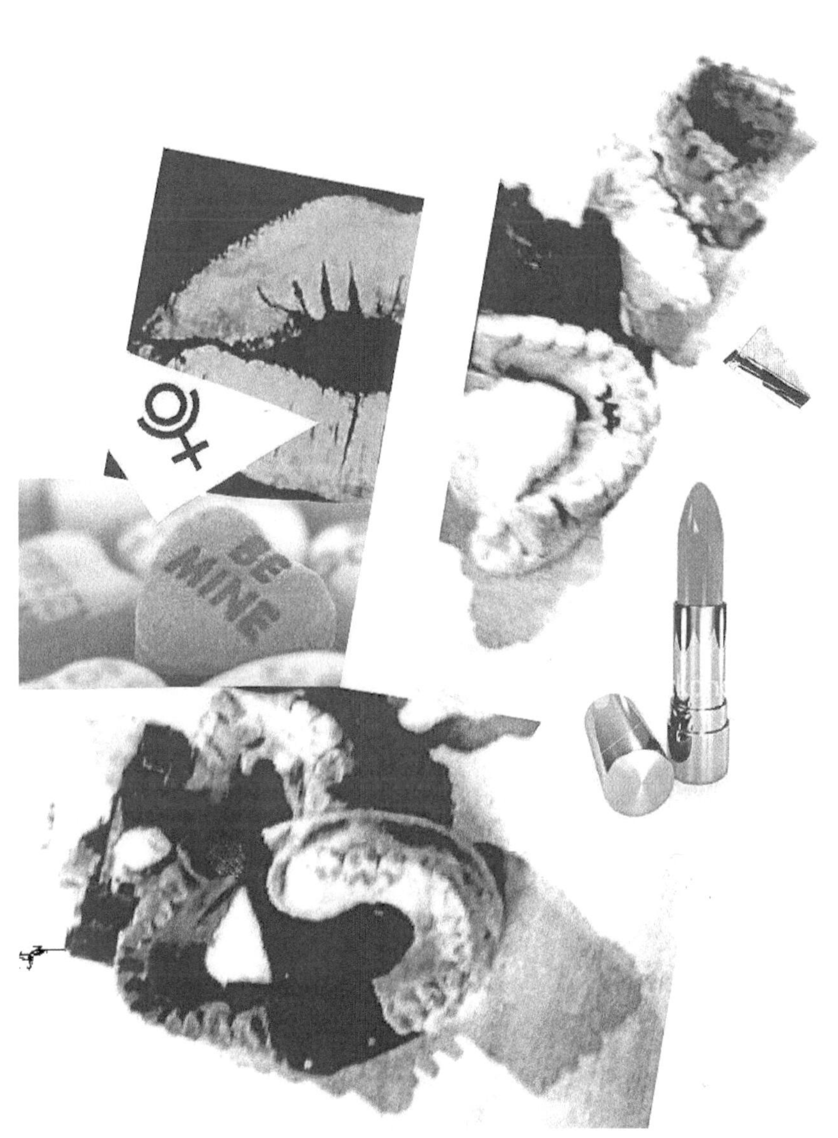
BE
MINE

Elektra's Mouth

i. (wherein she has her most recent kiss)

She doesn't like the way she smells. It feels to her as though someone else's smells have invaded her body. She has seen films or read stories about invasions of other consciousnesses, strange spirits stealing mortal bodies, alien implants, but never invading odors. Everything about her smells wrong, her feet, her breath, her farts, her vagina, her skin.

She has fallen in love, at least twice, with a lover's smell first, and other qualities she imagined they possessed later. A certain kind of body odor, the smell of a man who has spent hours welding, mixed with light musk and amber, causes her womb to involuntarily tighten, brings to her mouth the taste of longing, semen, satisfaction, caviar. She hears the sound of crystal hitting linoleum in a sharp high shower. Another body odor, the smell of a woman just out of ballet class, who had fucked just outside of class, having showered the night before, lathered with Dr. Bonner's peppermint soap, then rubbed herself with patchouli, sandalwood and rosemary oils, makes her feel a sleeping cat purring against her belly, her fingers gripping someone else's, woven together. Her mouth warms to the taste of potato soup, drums pound at the back of her throat.

She smells of decay. Her breath smells of her first cavity. Her vagina smells like every lover she ever had, and a few she only imagined. He has no smell at all. His breath tastes like nothing, not even the nothingness of purity, clear stream water, spring wind. No, he tastes of no thing.

They kiss. They have kissed before, small, chaste kisses, bodies held groins apart, barely touching hands to shoulders, longlegged insects dancing on still water. Now though, he pulls her to him, brings her belly to his by pressing his hand into her back. His forearm increases the pressure, while his palm, fingers pointing down, presses into her sacrum. His other hand hovers between her shoulder blades. It hesitates, rather than lingers, unmoving. He burns, but the heat cannot be felt outside his skin, even pressing against his skin. He is plastic logs in an electric fireplace, a videotape of a potbellied stove. She hates him for her relief.

ii. (wherein she has her first kiss)

It was twilight, and she was hiding in the tall grass behind the outdoor chapel, the one that reached out the cliff's edge to the ocean, a hand, palm cupped, reaching out to scoop up the water, a thirsty traveler. She sat hidden, writing in a small black book. She imagined herself a great poet, a wild romantic figure about whom novels would be written. Men would fall in love with her; write music for her, beg to paint her. He found her there, the sun hot against her back as it began to wade into the Pacific, dipping fingers in to test the water.

He was Paul Robbins, Helen Slade's boyfriend, fourteen, cool, blonde, blue-eyed, sure of himself. The sun glinted off his Tiger Beat curls, and he leaned in and pressed his lips to hers, surprising her. She hadn't known he was about to kiss her, hadn't known he had ever looked at her. She was Helen's best friend, and she had never been kissed. Helen and she had sat up for hours, talking about boys, along with the other girls in their cabin. Leslie Reynolds had gone to third base, had let a boy slide his finger inside her vagina. Helen talked about Paul slipping his tongue inside her mouth. Helen was very certain that this was the most disgusting thing that had ever happened, and was considering becoming a nun. Elektra was too busy feeling her vagina tighten to point out that Jews don't have nuns.

She wasn't particularly attracted to Paul, but when he kissed her she felt her body respond. The kiss lasted only a second, his tongue reaching out to flick against the edge of her lips, before he pulled away and disappeared down the hill. She curled up on her side on the ground, feeling her cut-offs pressing into her flesh, her fingers touching her barely open mouth, and almost heard the hiss of the sun sinking into the ocean behind, the sigh of the moon as it rose.

Paul didn't try to kiss her again that summer, and neither did any other boy, girlfriend or not. The last week of camp, the counselor she had a crush on took her aside and told her that there was talk that she had gone all the way. She flushed, heat rising from its home at her root up to her hairline, thinking 'of Paul's lips pressed against hers, of his tongue hesitating at the entrance to her mouth. She imagined her longing for more, for that tongue to reach back and meet her teeth, her tongue, to feel a chest, hard and hairless, pushing into her soft new breasts, to feel a hand other than her own touch that breast, to have the nipple harden in the tender valley where two fingers meet, and she felt shame fill her lungs. She was so aroused she couldn't speak, which the counselor assumed was an admission of guilt, walking off mumbling about girls' reputations.

In the fall, her first year of high school, she'd walk to school listening to Helen still talking about becoming a nun. Elektra stole her father's magazines from the bin beside his toilet, reading the letters and imagined herself a woman with lovers. She stole her mother's clothes, hoping creamy silk blouses made her look old enough to want. When she walked down the street outside of school, old men stared at her.

Now she was in the same school as Paul, still Helen's boyfriend, a sophomore. She and Helen parted in the hallway in front of their drama department lockers. Elektra turned the corner and bumped headlong into Paul, who grabbed her by the shoulders and pushed her up against the lockers. She could feel the lock on one pressing into her back as Paul brought his mouth to hers. His tongue paused at the edge of her lips, then forged ahead, scraping along her teeth inside her upper lip before forcing her teeth apart and finding her tongue. One hand moved from her shoulder to her breast, while the other hand pulled her face against his. The kiss lasted almost a minute. Then he backed away, saying nothing, and walked down the hall.

iii. (wherein her father observes an early kiss)

He had taken her to the Faire the first time she went, or more accurately, he took them, his pregnant wife and his not quite two-year-old daughter. It was 1965 that first time, and he was in love with them both. The heat of late spring in Agoura, bright sun lazy through the dust kicked up by crowds, shone on his daughter's blond curls, and he downed a beer in one gulp and lifted her to his shoulders.

Now, sixteen years later, almost nothing has changed in this time capsule of an Elizabethan village, filled with drunk men and buxom young girls, except now he comes alone with his wife, and the daughter works there.

After her first weekend working there, at a Sunday night Mother's Day dinner, he had to catch her when her legs gave out beneath her. He had mostly avoided touching her since her body became a duplicate of her Mother's. He had never wanted to intervene when his daughter became the focus of his wife's rage, could not bear to enter the electrical field of their interaction.

When he caught his daughter in his arms as she fell, he could smell her life, an ammonia capsule broken under his nose. She smelled of dust and hay, of beer and men, of cigarettes and strange perfume. He had ordered a drink at the bar while they waited for a Mother's Day table. Jack Daniel's, a double, on the rocks.

She worked at the back of the Faire, and it took more than an hour to wind through the crowds and find her booth, surrounded by a huge mass of people, some in Elizabethan costume, some dressed in their fantasy of a place that relies heavily on suspension of disbelief, enormous men in tights and Robin Hood hats, middle-aged women in chain mail bikinis.

The crowd formed a U at the bottom of the sloping hill. Beneath two large oaks, hay bales were stacked. Women stood on the bales, a choir, and, like a choir, they sang. He had seen her sing dozens of times, alone and with choirs, and he picked her out among the women easily, both from her voice, clear and bright, rising above the voices of the others, and from her glow. She was the youngest of the women, and his heart made a fist at how pretty she was, how she seemed lit up from the inside, skin smooth and pink, lips full, long hair curling down her back, honey gold in the sun.

In front of the hay bales there were two wooden Y's, tall as men. Men lined up beside them, where costumed attendants screamed out "three sponges for 100 pence." Men put the wet sponges, pulled dripping brown water and trailing bits of hay, into a sling tied between the two branches of the tall Y's. Pulling back, the sponges flew in a graceful arc hitting the women on the bales. A tall man and his friend talked loudly about aiming at the blond chick with the boobs, and he knew they were talking about his daughter. He took a sip of the beer he held, now warm from the heat of his hand, hotter than the l00-degree day, trying to wash away the taste of blood and bile from his mouth. The tall man's sponge landed on her cleavage with a sharp, wet smack, and she stepped down from the bales with the help of the women in front of her, jumping to the ground so her skirts rose with a puff of dusty air. She met the tall man in front of the bales, and his hands reached for her. Pulling her face to his, he leaned down, tongue first, and almost lifted her mouth so that it was impaled on his tongue. His daughter's mouth, his daughter's hair, his daughter's waist. He ducked below the crowd in front of him, hoping she couldn't see him.

iv. (wherein her father kisses water)

He was learning to water ski in the cool green water of Lake Arrowhead. He slid into the shallow area next to the dock, the clay of the bottom slipping between his toes, cooling the heat of the three bloody marys that had been breakfast. Pansy and

Petunia, the black dachshunds that belonged to the Slades, as the pier belonged to the Slades, and the boat, and the water skis, danced on the dock.

If the bloody marys had been spiked with mescaline, or psilocybin, or LSD, he might have liked the dachshunds better. He might have imagined them as being his own dogs, seen at a great distance. Seen at a great distance after someone spiked their

kibble with amphetamines. His dogs were also black, and shorthaired, but Claudia and Karma were Great Danes, giant, long powerful legged, dignified, everything Pansy and Petunia weren't.

He floated in the cool water, his back to the dock, feeling the water slip between his feet and the rubber of the envelope the skis held like baggy shoes, clown shoes. The boat prepared to move away, pulling him along, a shark cutting through cold, deep water, lampreys carried clinging to its side. In the last second, in the inhalation before a sneeze, Petunia leapt as high as tiny legs not designed for leaping would allow, and landed on his shoulders, a stole wrapping itself around his neck, a refugee, a stowaway.

His sister Fran had died at 34 without ever choosing her own clothes, her own friends. Even her dreams were dreamt by their mother first, and edited so that nothing fantastic, nothing erotic, no giant-breasted goddesses eating their young, no serpent-phallused goat gods, penises undulating and reaching, forked tongues spitting, could reach Fran in her sleep. Would you kill for freedom? Would you die for it? She did.

He didn't, except the parts of him that yearned, that lived only in the space made by the wind between feathers. He killed off the bits that can only breathe the oxygen in tears, in blood, in mud. He murdered the selves that had webbed feet, and extra nipples, and pointed ears.

His daughter's ears were pointed, so much so that the other children called her Mrs. Spock, and Martian, and Pluto. When she learned to water ski, the first time she fell, she held onto the rope, allowing herself to be pulled along quickly through the

water, under the water, as though she could let the water run through her until she softened and became liquid herself. It scared him to death, and he yelled his fear out, louder than the boat's diesel engines, louder than the yapping of the dogs, louder

than the voice of his mother in his head.

v. (wherein she reflects)

Mozzarella cheese is beautiful when it clings, hot and stringy, to the bread of a grilled cheese sandwich. Far superior to other cheeses, indifferent lovers, either melting haphazardly, flowing indiscriminately between bread and plate, plate and mouth, shapeless, formless, lacking intent, or separating into pools of unpalatable oil and perforated, chewy plastic, a gigolo, insincere and greasy. Her father only cooked one thing, and that restricted to the rare occasions when her mother wasn't around. Grilled cheese, mozzarella on sourdough, bread grilled in butter on both sides. The sticky mozzarella kept the sandwiches together to the last bite.

She has felt that, that longing for teeth that pull, desire to wrap around a tongue, to make a prisoner of it, before being swallowed, sliding down slippery dark hot throat. To be food instead of eating it. To fill, instead of waiting to be filled. She imagines being squeezed inside the power of a stomach, held close by the force of longing of the intestines, pulling, coaxing the contents of the stomach, already transformed by pressure and chemistry, into something else, something destined for other things, something horrible and beautiful.

Some people, when they are dying of thirst, drink their own urine. It is even fashionable to drink urine when you aren't dying of thirst. Some take it as a cure for cancer, for aging, for AIDS, as though consuming death keeps it away. A dog, when left without food, will eat its own shit. When we are hungry enough, we will eat anything, even each other. Especially each other.

Her father's family never told any stories. Not just no myths or fairy tales, they told no stories, of themselves, of each other, of anyone. His father never spoke the names of his two brothers, swallowed their names, died with them hidden in the curve of his colon, not even letting them out in death.

In the state of California, once a part of you has been cut off, or lost, or taken, it cannot be removed from hospital grounds. No matter that it was *once* your arm, your appendix, your womb, your unborn child; it is no longer yours once it is not in or on your body. You cannot give it a burial, or watch it burn, or preserve it and keep it in a jar on your mantle.

About the Author

Suzi Kaplan Olmsted is a two time **Puschart Prize** nominee, poet, author and illustrator. Suzi's work has appeared in publications such as *The Sun, Blue Satellite, 51%, F.T.S, Big Scream, M.A.G., poetrysuperhighway.com, Lummox Journal, getunderground.com* and *Napalm Health Spa*. Suzi also illustrated portions of **The Ellyn Maybe Coloring Book** and **Beatitude - Golden Anniversary 1959-2009**. Her first collection, **Institutional Wallet** was published in 2009 by Virgogray Press. Suzi Kaplan Olmsted resides in Oakland with her husband, poet Marc Olmsted.

These Titles Currently Available from Virgogray Press

NO FEAR by Doctori Sadisco

Carcinogenic Poetry Print Anthology Vol. 1

Nothing. No One. Nowhere. No. 2

In the Broken Things – Gillian Prew

Nothing. No One. Nowhere. No. 3

Vegas Implosions – Chris D'Errico

By the Banks of the Ajoy, Jaideb Vanishes into the Blue – Subhankar Das

www.virgograypress.com